I Can Do It!

I Can Tell Time

By Meg Gaertner

www.littlebluehousebooks.com

Copyright © 2023 by Little Blue House, Mendota Heights, MN 55120. All rights reserved. No part of this book may be reproduced or utilized in any form or by any means without written permission from the publisher.

Little Blue House is distributed by North Star Editions:
sales@northstareditions.com | 888-417-0195

Produced for Little Blue House by Red Line Editorial.

Photographs ©: Shutterstock Images, cover, 4, 6–7, 9, 10–11, 13, 14–15, 17, 19, 21, 22-23, 24 (top left), 24 (top right), 24 (bottom left), 24 (bottom right)

Library of Congress Control Number: 2022901677

ISBN
978-1-64619-581-7 (hardcover)
978-1-64619-608-1 (paperback)
978-1-64619-661-6 (ebook pdf)
978-1-64619-635-7 (hosted ebook)

Printed in the United States of America
Mankato, MN
082022

About the Author

Meg Gaertner enjoys reading, writing, dancing, and being outside. She lives in Minnesota.

Table of Contents

I Can Tell Time **5**

Glossary **24**

Index **24**

I Can Tell Time

The time is eight o'clock.

It is time to play.

The time is nine o'clock.

It is time to run.

run

The time is ten o'clock.

It is time to paint.

paint

The time is eleven o'clock.

It is time to read.

The time is one o'clock.

It is time to hug.

hug

13

The time is two o'clock.

It is time to laugh.

laugh

The time is three o'clock.

It is time to drink.

The time is six o'clock.

It is time to eat.

eat

19

The time is seven o'clock.

It is time to wash.

The time is eight o'clock.

It is time to sleep.

sleep

Glossary

drink

read

hug

sleep

Index

E
eat, 18

L
laugh, 14

P
play, 5

W
wash, 20